TIME-LIFE
Early Learning Program

# VOYAGE of the MICRONAUTS

TIME
LIFE *for*
*Children* ™

ALEXANDRIA, VIRGINIA

## Note to Parents

*Voyage of the Micronauts* is designed to teach your child all about the human body. It details the adventures of four microscopic visitors from the planet Xeno, who come to Earth for a close-up look at a human being. After flying around an eight-year-old soccer player named Freddy, the Micronauts experience engine failure and wind up touring the inside of Freddy's body as well.

In order to appeal to children of differing ages, the book functions both as an adventure story and as an introduction to basic human anatomy. To make this topic more accessible, several special features have been included. Fact boxes use a question-and-answer format to convey information about physical attributes, the senses, and behavior. Maps track the ship's progress through the interior, and diagrams explain how various parts of the human body work.

## Part I: We Go Exploring

The *Microsphere*, an explorer craft from the planet Xeno, hurtled through space.

"Entering Earth's atmosphere," called out Navigator Marko.

"We're about to explore a real earthling!" whispered 10-year-old Rikki to Rokko, her seven-year-old brother.

"Frabbid!" replied Rokko. ("Frabbid" is the Xenite word for "awesome.")

"We land in 30 seconds," said Commander Demi.

Rikki and Rokko peered out the viewport. The ship hovered above a big green field. Earthlings darted about the field, kicking a black-and-white sphere.

"Which earthling shall we explore, Commander?" asked Marko.

Commander Demi pointed to a boy who stood in
front of some white posts.

"The one over there who's standing still," she said.
"He'll be easier to land on."

With a big "WHOOOSH!" the spaceship flew down...down...down to the top of the boy's head. The *Microsphere* was so tiny that the boy could not feel it land.

## Frabbid Facts

### Why do some earthlings have freckles?

Because their skin contains little clumps of a special coloring called melanin. The melanin is there to protect the earthling's skin from the harmful ultraviolet rays of the sun. As the earthling grows older, his or her freckles often go away.

The ship came to rest in a tangled forest.

"We've landed on top of the earthling boy," said Demi, "in the middle of a covering that humans call 'hair.' He has about 300,000 hairs! Their job is to protect the head."

Demi sent out the Robotic Sampling Scissors, which snipped some hair and brought it back into the ship.

"This is a bit of the earthling's hair," she reported.

"Why didn't he feel anything when you cut it?" asked Rokko.

"Because only the very bottom part of each hair is alive," said Demi. "That's why it doesn't hurt when he gets his hair cut, but is does hurt when a hair gets pulled out."

Rikki rubbed her own bald head.

"Things are getting pretty hairy around here," she said. "Let's go somewhere else!"

★ **Xenite** ★

**Locator Map**

You are here

The Hair

**Earthling Boy**

Quick as a gnat, the *Microsphere* whizzed down to the boy's eyes, which were moving back and forth. The ship moved along with his eyes until Rikki said, "I'm getting dizzy! Why are his eyes moving around like that?"

"Because he's watching the other earthlings," said Demi.

## Why do humans blink?

They blink to clean their eyes. Each eye has a movable cover, called an eyelid, that acts like a windshield wiper. The eyelid uses the wetness in the eye to help wipe away any dirt that gets on the surface. Humans blink about every six seconds, all day long.

Suddenly a cloud passed in front of the sun. A shadow covered the field, and the black part in the center of the boy's eye grew larger.

"What's going on?" asked Rokko.

"It just got darker outside," said Demi, "so the pupil—that black circle in the middle of his eye—got bigger to let in more light."

When the sun shone bright again, the black circle in the boy's eye grew smaller.

"Now the day is brighter," said Demi. She and Rokko looked at a diagram. "His pupil has become smaller again to shut out some of the light and protect the sensitive inside part of his eye."

"I hear you," said Rokko, nodding his understanding.

"That reminds me!" said Demi. "Next stop...the ear!"

## Frabbid Facts

### How do humans see?

With two complex sensors called eyes. When light bounces off a butterfly, for example, it enters the eye through the pupil and is focused on the back of the eye by the lens. The back of the eye sends this upside-down picture of the butterfly to the brain, which turns it right side up again.

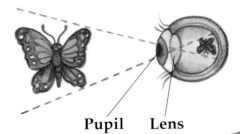

Pupil    Lens

Cloudy Day

Sunny Day

The *Microsphere* stopped beside a huge cave in the
side of a cliff.

"We've reached his ear," announced Commander Demi.
"The outside is shaped like a funnel to pick up sounds
that travel through the air."

"Let's make a noise he can hear!" cried Rokko.

"I'll try!" said Demi. She pressed a few buttons, and a
horn rose from the top of the spaceship.

"HON-N-N-K-K-K!!!" The horn let out such a loud blast that
the Micronauts were thrown backward. The boy didn't budge.

"No wonder he couldn't hear that," said Demi, studying a book called *Guide to Humans*. "The loudest sound this horn makes can be heard by a dog, but not by a human. Dogs hear much better than people."

"Well, then," suggested Rikki, "let's go explore a dog!" (Rikki loved animals of all types, whatever planet they lived on.)

"No time for that!" said Demi.

Marko revved the ship's engines, and the Xenites zoomed off again.

**Guide to Humans**

**Frabbid Facts**

The ear picks up sound traveling through the air and funnels it down a tube (1) to the eardrum (2), a thin sheet of skin stretched tight like a drum. The eardrum begins to vibrate, or move rapidly back and forth. Three tiny bones (3) and a special coil (4) change the vibrations into signals and send them to the brain, which tells the earthling what noise he or she is hearing.

The *Microsphere* traveled around the boy's body until it came to a vast surface covered with tiny hairs.

"This is the biggest organ in the boy's body," Demi said to the Xenite children. "Do you know what it's called?"

Rikki and Rokko exchanged puzzled glances.

"It's the skin!" answered Demi. "The boy's skin helps hold his body together. It also keeps the liquids inside his body from drying out."

★ **Xenite** ★

**Locator Map**

You are here

**The Arm**

**The Skin**

**Earthling Boy**

"Wow!" said Rokko. "Can his skin do anything else?"

"It sure can!" Demi told him. "For one thing, it's waterproof! That means it keeps the water out of his body when he goes swimming, or when he takes a bath. His skin also produces sweat, which cools him off when he gets hot.

"Let's check the Didjano Database for more information," Demi suggested. She tapped her keyboard and the computer screen flickered to life:

### Did You Know...?

...that fingernails are actually hardened skin? Their job is to protect the fingertips and toes.

...that an eight-year-old child can sweat more than three quarts of water in a single day? To replace this lost liquid, kids need to drink plenty of water in hot weather.

...that it takes 200,000 frowns to make one wrinkle on a human's face? To avoid wrinkles, an earthling should avoid frowns!

Suddenly the explorers heard a high-pitched buzzing: "ZZZZZ!"  They rushed to the viewport and saw a living helicopter armed with a large needle.

"Whoa!" cried Rikki and Rokko.  They watched as the strange thing landed on the boy's skin and pricked it with the needle.

"Let's bug out of here!" cried Demi.

The little ship got out of the way just in time. The boy slapped his skin, crushing the helicopter. Then he rubbed his fingers back and forth over his skin.

"What happened?" asked Rikki.

"The boy was bitten by a mosquito," said Demi. "It's an insect that lives on blood!"

The Micronauts stared in astonishment as a big bump rose up on the boy's skin.

"His skin is reacting to the bite," Demi explained. "But don't worry—that bug was only big enough to take a tiny sip of blood."

"Where to now?" asked Marko.

Demi looked in a notebook called *The Interplanetary Trip Planner.* "To his hands!" she replied.

At that moment, the soccer ball came sailing through the air toward the boy. His teammates shouted, "Catch it, Freddy!" The boy lifted his arms and caught the ball with both hands.

**Frabbid Facts**

**Without thumbs, a human would not be able to:**

Brush her teeth with a toothbrush;
Tie his shoes;
Eat cereal with a spoon;
Hold a pencil or a crayon;
Snap her fingers;
Turn a doorknob;
Shake hands;
Throw or catch a baseball;
Thumb through a picture book.

"How was Freddy able to catch that black-and-white orb?" asked Rokko.
"By using something that most other animals on Earth don't have—thumbs!" said Demi. "Humans can touch their thumbs to their fingers, so they can use tools and hold onto all sorts of things, like that sphere they call a 'soccer ball.' "

With a strong throw, Freddy hurled the soccer ball to one of his teammates.

"How does he bend his arm like that?" Rikki asked.

"There's a joint called an 'elbow' in the middle of his arm," said Demi.

"Like a hinge on a door, the elbow joint lets the arm bend in one direction only."

"Zybergoid!" cried Rokko. ("Zybergoid" is Xenite for "amazing.")

"But how does the elbow work?"

"Send out the x-ray camera!" Demi instructed Marko.

A special camera popped out from the side of the *Microsphere*. It took a picture of Freddy's elbow and displayed it on the ship's computer.

"Let's put on our x-ray specs for a better look!" said Demi. The other explorers gathered around.

"As you can see, the elbow is the place where the bones in the upper and lower parts of Freddy's arm fit together."

**Radius**

**Humerus**

**Ulna**

**Elbow Joint**

"Are those the only bones in his body?" asked Rikki.

"Not by a long shot!" said Demi. "He's got nearly 300 bones in all!"

Demi turned to Marko and said, "We need a full-body view—reel in the camera!"

Marko moved the camera back toward the ship and snapped an x-ray photograph of Freddy's body from head to toe.

Pointing to the picture on the screen, Demi explained, "The bones form a framework that supports the entire body."

"Are they hard or soft?" asked Rokko.

"Both!" replied Demi. "Bones are hard on the outside but soft on the inside."

## Frabbid Facts

### What happens when a bone breaks?

When a bone gets broken, a doctor has to rejoin its damaged parts. The bone must then be held in place so that it cannot move; to do this, the doctor puts a stiff white cast on the body part that contains the broken bone. (For a reason that Xenite scientists do not yet understand, young earthlings like to write and draw funny things on the hardened cast.) During the next four to eight weeks, the broken parts of the bone knit, or grow, back together again.

"Do his bones make him move?" Rikki wondered.

"No," said Demi, "but the things that help him move are attached to his bones—they're called muscles."

"This," Marko proclaimed, "calls for a digigram!" (That's Xenite for "digital diagram.") He tapped some keys on his computer, and a chart of the muscles in Freddy's arm slid down from the ceiling.

**Muscle Bundle**

**Muscle Cell (enlarged)**

**Frabbid Facts**

## How does a muscle cell work?

Every muscle cell in the human body has the power to contract—that is, to make itself shorter—and then relax. When the earthling wants to move, his brain sends a message to a bundle of his muscle cells; the cells in the bundle contract, working together to pull his bones in the direction he wants them to go.

Demi pointed to the digigram and said, "These are just a few of the 630 muscles that Freddy has in his body. Each muscle is made up of millions of tiny cells."

"Sails?" said Rokko. "I love solar sailing—show me the sails!"

"*Cells*, Rokko, not sails!" Demi corrected him. "They're the building blocks of all living matter, but they're so small you need a microscope to see them. Freddy's body has a grand total of about six billion—that's 6,000,000,000—muscle cells!"

Just then, the ball came rolling quickly along the ground toward the goal. Freddy made a diving save and stopped it just in time. But he scraped his knee when he hit the ground, and the cut began to bleed.

"Uh-oh!" said Marko. "Looks like Freddy has been injured!"

"We'll need a damage report," said Demi. "Fly down to his knees!"

As the *Microsphere* hovered beside Freddy's cut knee, Rikki asked, "What's that red stuff?"

"That's a tiny bit of the blood that moves through his body," said Demi. "Usually it stays inside, but when he cuts his skin, some of the blood comes out."

"Why doesn't *all* of his blood come out?" Rokko wondered.

"Because the human body is such an incredible machine that it can fix itself!" said Demi. "First the blood clots—that means it gets thicker—around the cut. Then a special patch, called a scab, will grow over Freddy's cut; once the skin underneath it has healed, the scab will fall off."

"BUR-R-R-E-E-E-P!"
A whistle sounded, and all the earthlings suddenly stopped chasing the ball. Freddy trotted across the field toward the sideline.
"Let's fly over there and see what he's up to," suggested Marko.

When the Xenites caught up with Freddy, he was holding a fresh orange slice. Suddenly, his nostrils flared wide open.

"Why are those flaps wiggling like that?" Rokko asked.

"Those aren't flaps," said Demi. "They're nostrils. They're part of his nose, and he opens them wider when he's trying to smell something."

"What else is his nose good for?" asked Rikki.

"It warms the air he breathes, and it keeps out dust, dirt, and other things that might make him choke."

"He's about to put that orange thing in his mouth!" cried Rikki.

"A golden opportunity!" said Demi. "Let's fly down for a closer look!"

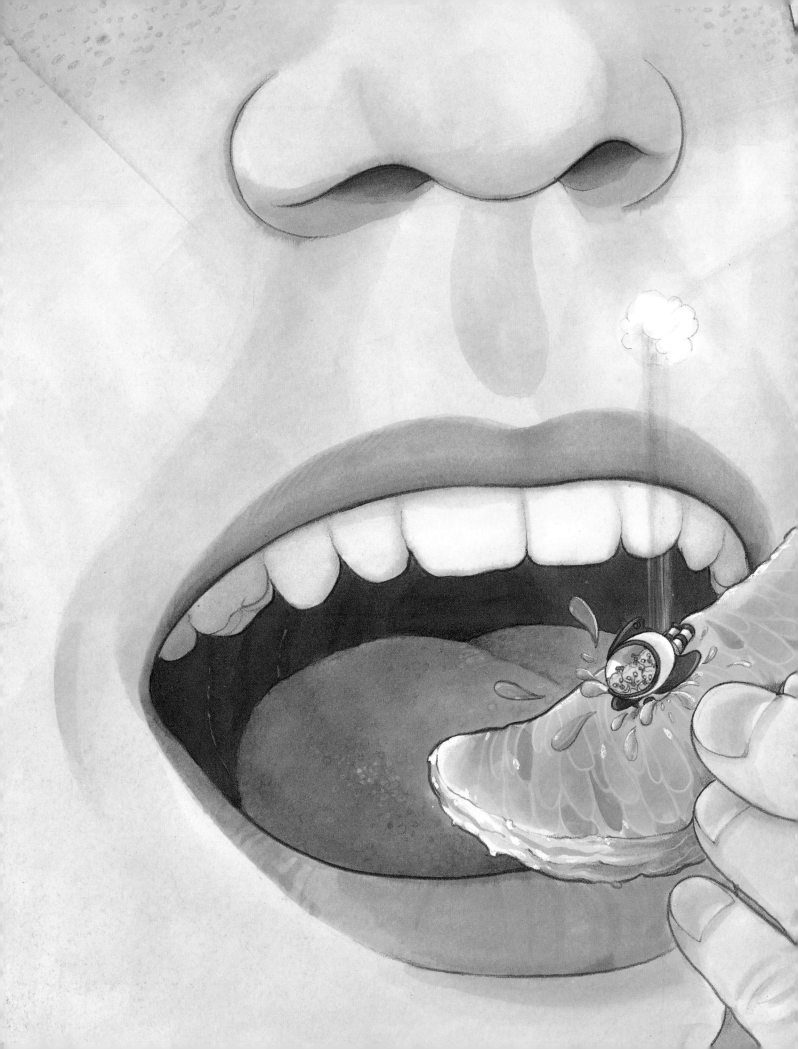

As the *Microsphere* hovered above the orange slice, an alarm suddenly went off on the ship's control panel.

"Ow-*OOO*-gah!  Ow-*OOO*-gah!"

"Engine failure!" shouted Marko.  "We're losing altitude! Prepare for a crash landing!"

The *Microsphere* dropped onto the orange—just as Freddy put it in his mouth!

## Part II: A Detour through Freddy

Darkness surrounded the Xenites.

"Where are we?" Rokko wondered.

"We're taking an unscheduled side trip inside the human body!" said Demi. "We'll just have to make the best of it."

Emergency lights clicked on inside and outside the ship.

"We're in Freddy's mouth," Demi reported.

"He's using his tongue, his teeth, and a liquid called saliva to turn the bites of that sweet orange into tiny lumps so that his body can use the food for energy."

"Will we get chewed up too?" worried Rokko.

"No," Demi assured him. "We're too small for that!"

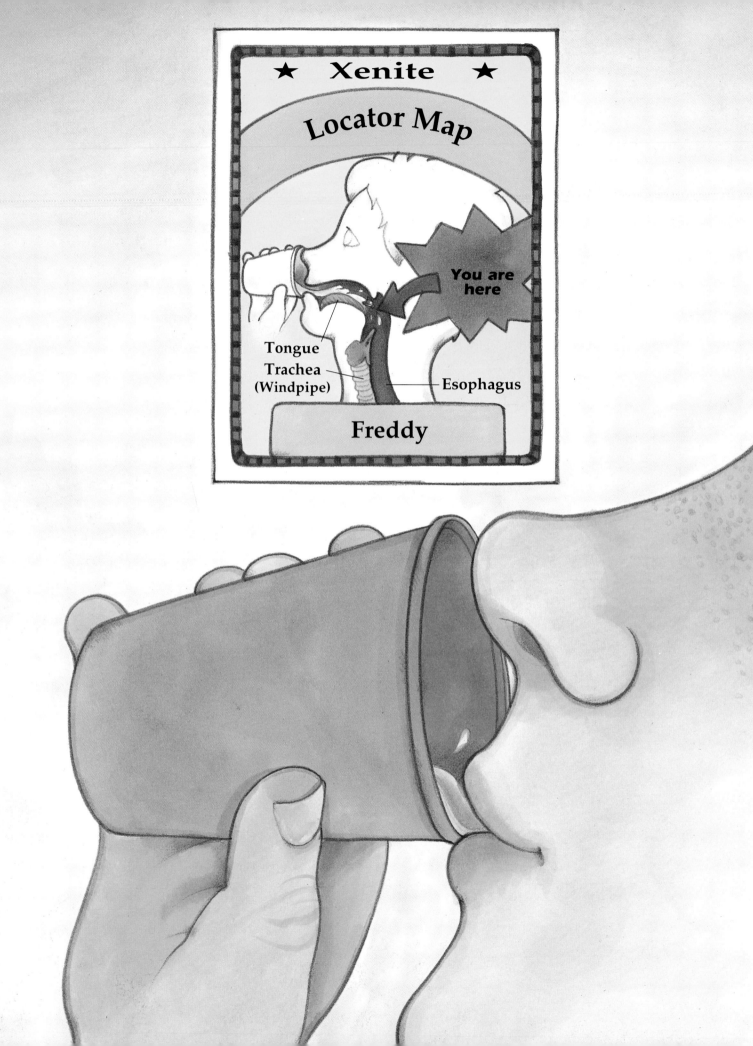

The Micronauts caught a glimpse of daylight as Freddy briefly opened his mouth. Then he closed his lips around the rim of a cup, and a clear liquid came pouring in. The *Microsphere* began to float on the liquid.

"Oh, no!" cried Demi. "He's drinking water! We'll be washed down his esophagus!"

"His e-*what*-igus?" yelled Rikki and Rokko at the same time.

"His e*soph*agus!" Demi called back. "It's a tube that goes from his throat to his stomach. The muscles in the tube tighten and loosen one after another to push food—and us!—down into his stomach."

After a wild ride down the esophagus, the *Microsphere* landed with a plop in a gigantic pool.

"We're inside Freddy's stomach!" announced Demi. "The walls of his stomach are sending out special juices, called acids, that mix with the food he's eaten and break it down into smaller pieces. Marko, activate the acid shields!"

"Roger, Chief!" said Marko. A strange device emerged from the top of the *Microsphere* and sprayed a protective coating over the outside of the ship.

★ Xenite
Locator Map
★

Mouth

Esophagus

You are here

Stomach

Large Intestine

Small Intestine

Colon

The Digestive System

### Did You Know...?

...that the "growling" noise made by an empty stomach is the sound of gas being squeezed against the stomach walls? The official earthling word for this noise— "borborygmus"—is a real mouthful!

...that it takes five to six hours for the stomach to fully digest a meal? To prevent the hunger pangs caused by an empty stomach, humans must eat three meals a day.

...that an empty stomach is as skinny as a hot dog? When full, the stomach can get as big as a one–quart milk carton!

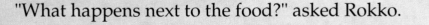

"What happens next to the food?" asked Rokko.

"The small pieces stay in his stomach until they become a liquid," Demi answered. "Then, like water swirling down the drain of a bathtub, the liquid goes through an opening at the bottom of his stomach and into a long tube called the small intestine."

"Testing?" cried Rokko. "What testing? I thought you said no homework on this trip!"

Before Demi could clear up the confusion, the *Microsphere* went into a dizzy dive. As it spiraled downward, the explorers all shouted out, "Here we go-o-o-o-o!"

"We've entered the small intestine!" Marko reported.

"Now *that's* an absorbing topic!" said Demi. "It's here that tiny bits of food—the ones the body can use for energy—move into the bloodstream."

"The bloodstream?" said Rikki. "Would that be a way out of Freddy's body?"

"It's worth a try!" said Demi. "But first we'll have to get as small as a molecule of water. Marko, shrink the ship!"

ZZZHEEEROOOP!

The *Microsphere* shrank to a fraction of its former size. The next instant, the ship was sucked through the wall of the small intestine and into Freddy's bloodstream.

The Micronauts found themselves traveling at high speed through a tiny tube filled with Freddy's blood.

"Mooga-looga!" shouted Rokko. (That's Xenite for "We're flying now!")

He pressed his nose to the glass and watched red and white saucers whizzing by outside.

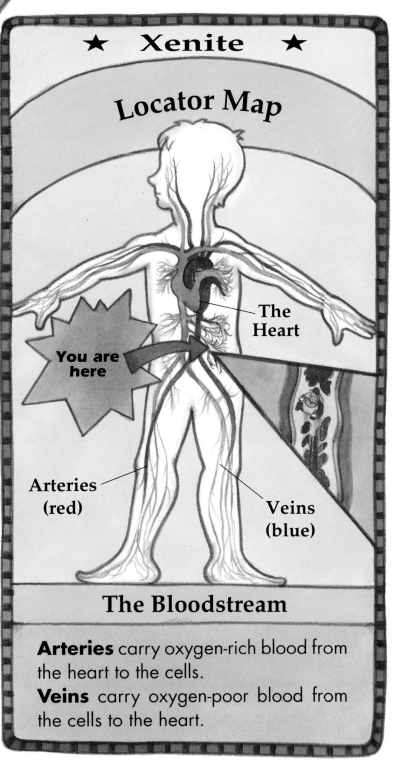

## ★ Xenite ★

### Locator Map

The Heart

**You are here**

Arteries
(red)

Veins
(blue)

### The Bloodstream

**Arteries** carry oxygen-rich blood from the heart to the cells.
**Veins** carry oxygen-poor blood from the cells to the heart.

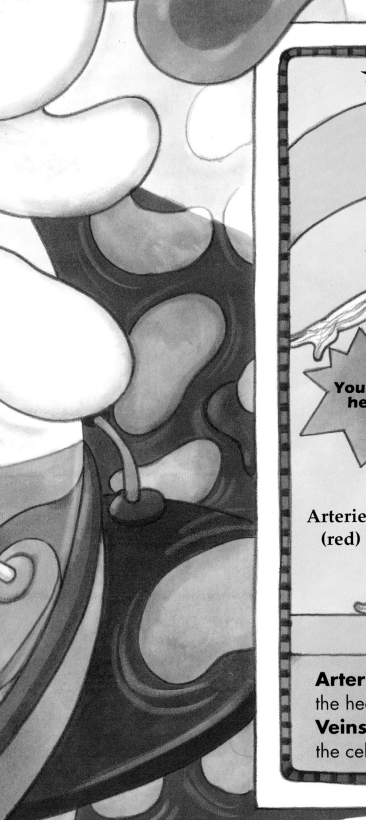

"What are those things?" Rokko wondered.

"The red discs are red blood cells," Demi explained. "They carry food and oxygen to the muscles, the bones, and every other part of Freddy's body."

"And the white ones?" asked Rikki.

"The white discs are white blood cells," said Demi. "Their job is to fight disease and infections, and—uh-oh!"

Crunch!  MUNCH!!  **SCURRR-UNCH!!!**
The *Microsphere* was under attack!  White blood cells
had glommed onto the ship and were trying to gobble it up!
"Oh, no!" cried Demi.  "Those white blood cells think we're
a germ—they're trying to get rid of us!  Send out the Boppers!"

Thirteen mechanical hands popped out of the *Microsphere* and bopped the white blood cells away.

"That was a close call!" said Demi. "I know those white blood cells are supposed to protect Freddy, but they nearly put an end to us! We'd better keep moving!"

Far in the distance, but steadily growing closer, the Xenites could hear a rhythmic thumping:

"Lub-DUB!  Lub-DUB!  Lub-DUB!"

"Oh, no!" groaned Rikki and Rokko.  "*Now* what's the matter?"

"Don't worry," Demi told them.  "That's just the sound of Freddy's heart pumping blood all through his body.  His heart is one of the things that keeps him alive.  It stays hard at work even when he's sleeping!"

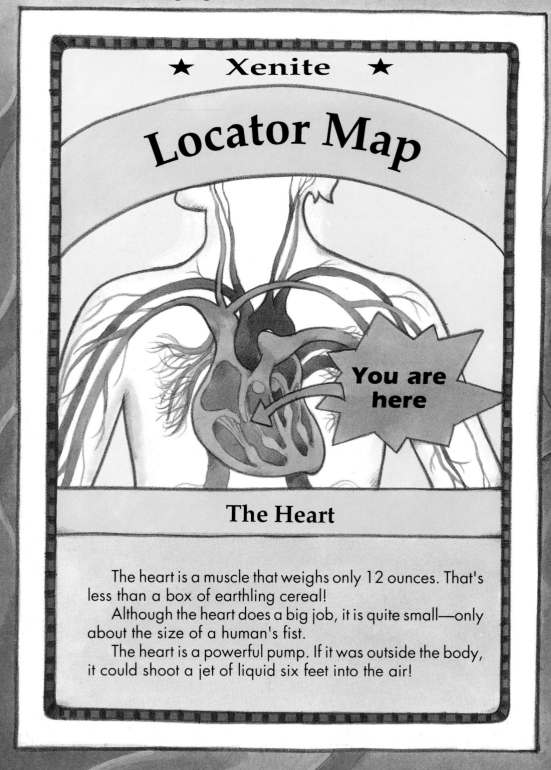

★ Xenite ★

# Locator Map

You are here

## The Heart

The heart is a muscle that weighs only 12 ounces. That's less than a box of earthling cereal!

Although the heart does a big job, it is quite small—only about the size of a human's fist.

The heart is a powerful pump. If it was outside the body, it could shoot a jet of liquid six feet into the air!

The *Microsphere* entered Freddy's heart and began to shake, rattle, and roll. "Whew!" cried Rokko. "All this bouncing around is making me thirsty! Let's take a bongleberry juice break!" (Bongleberries are huge fruits that grow all over the planet Xeno; to pick one, you just shout "Bongle!" and it drops to the ground.) Rokko took four juice boxes out of the ship's refrigerator and passed them around. When everyone had taken a sip, Rikki asked, "How does the heart work?" "Here," said Demi, handing her juice box to Rokko. "Hold my drink for a microsecond and I'll explain it to you."

Rikki gripped the box too hard, and bongleberry juice came squirting out of the straw. (Even aliens have a hard time handling a full juice box.)

"That's it!" cried Demi.

"That's what?" asked Rikki.

"That's exactly how the heart works!" said Demi. "The heart muscle pumps blood through a tube called the aorta the same way your hand squeezed juice through that straw. The aorta is a blood vessel just like the one we've been traveling through, only much bigger."

The *lub-DUBs* were getting faster now.

"Freddy's heart has started beating more quickly," said Demi. "I'll bet he's breathing harder, too. This calls for the Transparentizer!"

Looking right through Freddy's body, the Transparentizer showed them that the boy was no longer playing goalie. Instead, he was dribbling the ball down the field at top speed. And just as Demi had predicted, Freddy was breathing harder with every step he took.

"Should we check out his lungs?" Rikki suggested.

"That would be a breath of fresh air!" answered Demi.

So the *Microsphere* made its way out of Freddy's heart and headed for his lungs.

As soon as the ship left Freddy's bloodstream and entered his right lung, strong winds began to blow the Micronauts about.

"That's a whale of a gale out there!" cried Rikki. "What in the galaxy is going on?"

"Nothing special," replied Demi in a calm voice. "That wind is just the air going in and out of Freddy's lungs as he breathes."

Meanwhile, back on the soccer field, Freddy was trying to catch his breath. His chest rose and fell as his lungs sucked in air and pushed it out again.

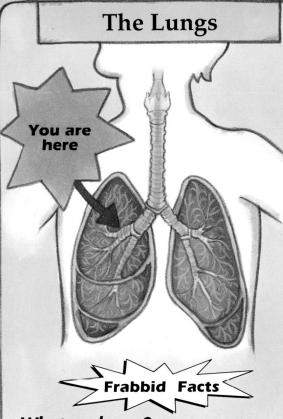

## The Lungs

**You are here**

### Frabbid Facts

**What are lungs?**

They are two inflatable sacs in the upper part of the chest. Together, the two lungs of an adult hold as much air as a basketball!

When a human breathes in, the lungs take a gas called oxygen out of the air and put it in the blood. The blood carries the oxygen to cells all over the body, which use it for energy. As the cells use the oxygen, they make a waste gas called carbon dioxide; the lungs get rid of this gas when the human breathes out.

From outside the ship came a disturbing sound: Spring! SPRANG!! SPROI-I-I-NGGG!!!

"Bad news!" reported Marko. "Freddy's breath has knocked our antenna loose!"

"Oh, no!" said Rikki. "Now we can't even phone home!"

"No problem!" said Demi. "A spacewalk will take care of everything!"

Rokko helped Marko into his spacesuit. Then Rikki opened the hatch and Marko stepped outside. He was spacewalking inside Freddy's lung!

The blasts of air going in and out of Freddy's lung made it hard for Marko to reach the broken antenna.  He checked the Windsockometer on his wrist.  "Wow! This air is moving past me at 10 miles per hour!  Freddy's lungs must be trying to get extra oxygen into his bloodstream to help him run faster!"  Just then, a gust of wind sent Marko hurtling deep into Freddy's lung!

Marko found himself flattened against the inner wall of a spongy little balloon called an alveolus.

"This is fantastic!" he said. "I've read about these alveoli—the lungs have 600 million of them! They're the places where oxygen gets traded for carbon dioxide!"

Before Marko could explore the alveolus any further, Freddy breathed out again, and Marko was sent flying back toward the *Microsphere*. As he sailed past the ship, he grabbed onto it with both hands. Then he fixed the broken antenna and scrambled inside.

"Woo-ee!" yelled Marko. "That was a close call! Which gives me an idea: Let's call the home planet and see if they know what to do!"

"Xenites calling Xeno!" Demi barked into the transmitter. "Come in, please!"

The radio crackled with static. "Xeno to Xenites!" came the garbled reply. "State your status!"

"We're trying to get out of a human body!" said Demi. "Right now we're in the lung! Can you help us?"

"Go to his command center!" the radio responded. There was another burst of static, and the radio went dead.

"His command center?" asked Marko. "Now what did they mean by that?"

"I think I know," said Demi, studying her map of the human body. "They want us to head for his brain!"

"Vranchi koo-lanna!" said Rokko. (That means "Xeno, here we come!") "I love to travel by train!"

"Not his *train*," cried Rikki, "his *brain!*" (Even siblings from distant worlds like to correct each other.)

With a roar of its tiny engines, the *Microsphere* left Freddy's lung and went back into his bloodstream. After another rollicking trip through his heart, the ship was pumped up a blood vessel to his brain.

**The Brain**

"Now arriving at the brain!" Marko announced.

Rikki and Rokko stared in astonishment at the gooey gray landscape outside. The brain was covered with deep grooves and high ridges, making it look like a cooked cauliflower.

"This is the command center for Freddy's body," Demi told the crew. "The brain gives the order to jump, run, sleep, giggle, feel love for family and friends, scratch, think, ask questions, breathe, eat, and—oh yes!—to remember!"

"Send out the monitor!" Demi commanded. "It will tell us where to go."

A robotic arm unfolded from the side of the *Microsphere* and placed a tiny monitor on the surface of Freddy's brain. Right away, it began flashing the word "Windpipe."

"Quick!" Demi told Marko. "Take us to Freddy's windpipe!"

"What's in it for us?" asked Rokko.

"A way out!" Demi replied. "Freddy's brain must be about to order him to open his mouth. When that happens, we'll fire our rockets, enlarge the ship, and zoom home!"

**Windpipe**

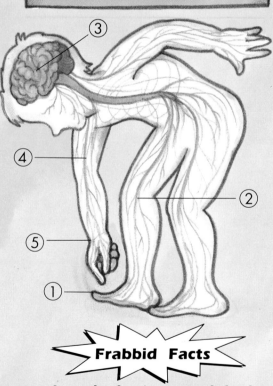

## The Nervous System

### Frabbid Facts

**How does the brain control the body?**

By sending messages over long, thin cables called nerves. If Freddy gets an itch on his toe (1), the message "itchy toe" travels up a nerve (2) to his brain (3). His brain sends the message "scratch toe" down a nerve (4) to his hand (5), which scratches his toe.

As the *Microsphere* traveled from Freddy's brain to his windpipe, excitement was building on the field. The game was tied 2-2. Only 30 seconds were left to play. And Freddy was dribbling the ball toward the other team's goal!

Along one sideline, everyone was cheering Freddy on: "Fred-*dee*! Fred-*dee*!" Their cries made him run even faster.

Two defensive players charged the ball. Freddy ran between them. Then he fired a shot that flew over the goalie and into the net.

Freddy had scored the winning goal!

Just then, Freddy opened his mouth and let loose the loudest holler of his life: "YA-A-A-AY!!!"

"I see light at the end of that tunnel!" Rokko shouted. "Let's make a break for it!"

Marko revved the ship's engines, and the *Microsphere* soared up and out of Freddy's body. The Xenites were free at last!

As Freddy celebrated the soccer victory with his teammates, the Micronauts flew back toward Xeno.

"Wow!" said Rokko. "I can't wait to tell my friends Sokko and Blokko about the way those frabbid blood cells attacked our ship!"

"Yeah!" agreed Rikki. "And wait 'til my friends Tikki and Mikki find out that I was in a human heart!"

Demi and Marko just traded happy looks. They were too tired even to mutter, "Vranchi koo-lanna." But each of them felt it from the tips of their toes to the tops of their bright blue boingers.

**TIME-LIFE for CHILDREN**™

*Publisher:* Robert H. Smith
*Associate Publisher/Managing Editor:* Neil Kagan
*Editorial Directors:* Jean Burke Crawford,
  Patricia Daniels, Allan Fallow, Karin Kinney, Sara Mark
*Editorial Coordinator:* Elizabeth Ward
*Director of Marketing:* Margaret Mooney
*Product Manager:* Cassandra Ford
*Assistant Product Manager:* Shelley L. Schimkus
*Director of Finance:* Lisa Peterson
*Assistant Business Manager:* Patricia Vanderslice
*Production Manager:* Prudence G. Harris
*Administrative Assistant:* Rebecca C. Christoffersen
*Special Contributor:* Jacqueline A. Ball


Produced by Joshua Morris Publishing, Inc.
Wilton, Connecticut 06897.
*Series Director:* Michael J. Morris
*Creative Director:* William N. Derraugh
*Editor:* Lynn Offerman
*Illustrator:* Tom Cooke
*Author:* Deborah Kovacs
*Designers:* Nora Voutas, Marty Heinritz
*Design Consultant:* Francis G. Morgan

CONSULTANTS

**Dr. Perri Klass,** a pediatrician in Boston, is the author of the novel *Other Women's Children*. She also wrote *A Not Entirely Benign Procedure*, an account of her four years at medical school, and *Baby Doctor*, a chronicle of her experiences as a pediatrician.

**Dr. Lewis P. Lipsitt,** an internationally recognized specialist on childhood development, was the 1990 recipient of the Nicholas Hobbs Award for science in the service of children. He serves as science director for the American Psychological Association and is a professor of psychology and medical science at Brown University, where he is director of the Child Study Center.

**Dr. Judith A. Schickedanz,** an authority on the education of preschool children, is an associate professor of early childhood education at the Boston University School of Education, where she also directs the Early Childhood Learning Laboratory. Her published work includes *More Than the ABC's: Early Stages of Reading and Writing Development* as well as several textbooks and many scholarly papers.

First printing. Printed in Hong Kong.
Published simultaneously in Canada.

Time Life Inc. is a wholly owned subsidiary of THE TIME INC. BOOK COMPANY.

TIME-LIFE is a trademark of Time Warner Inc. U.S.A.

Time Life Inc. offers a wide range of fine publications, including home video products. For subscription information, call 1-800-621-7026, or write TIME-LIFE BOOKS, P.O. Box C-32068, Richmond, Virginia 23261-2068.

**Library of Congress Cataloging-in-Publication Data**
Voyage of the micronauts.

    p. cm. – (Time-Life early learning program)
    Summary: While studying the exterior of an eight-year-old Earth boy from their tiny spaceship, four aliens from the planet Xeno are accidentally swallowed by him and get to observe the inside of his body and how it works.

    ISBN 0-8094-9295-4 (trade)   ISBN 0-8094-9296-2 (lib. bdg.)

    [1. Body, Human–Fiction. 2. Extraterrestrial beings–Fiction. 3. Science fiction.] I. Time-Life for Children (Firm) II. Series. PZ7.V9834 1992 [E]–dc20                                              91-29375
                                                                                  CIP
                                                                                   AC